STATES OF MIND

I FEEL GROUCHY

BY STEPHANIE FINNE

BLUE OWL BOOKS

TIPS FOR CAREGIVERS

Social and emotional learning (SEL) helps children manage emotions, create and achieve goals, maintain relationships, learn how to feel empathy, and make good decisions. The SEL approach will help children establish positive habits in communication, cooperation, and decision-making. By incorporating SEL in early reading, children will be better equipped to build confidence and foster positive peer networks.

BEFORE READING

Talk to the reader about his or her feelings. Talk about the different emotions and moods he or she may have.

Discuss: How do you know when you are happy or sad? How do you know when you are grouchy? What happens when that emotion lasts for a while?

AFTER READING

Talk to the reader about how he or she can manage being grouchy.

Discuss: What steps can you take when you are in a bad mood? What things help you deal with difficult emotions?

SEL GOAL

Some students may struggle with successfully regulating their emotions, thoughts, and behaviors. Help readers practice emotional intelligence skills so they can better identify their emotions and respond to them. How can they manage stress and bad moods such as grouchiness? How can they motivate themselves? Discuss how learning to do these things can help them manage their emotions.

TABLE OF CONTENTS

CHAPTER 1

FEELING GROUCHY

Do you ever wake up cranky? If something goes wrong, does it make you grouchy? Does your grumpy feeling stick around for a while?

When an **emotion** lasts longer than a few minutes, it is a **mood**. A mood can last several hours or even days. Grouchiness is a bad mood.

Annabel woke up grouchy this morning. She doesn't feel like playing. She doesn't even want to watch her favorite show. No matter what she tries, she feels grouchy. Her bad mood lasts all day.

Grouchiness can feel like sadness, **anxiety**, or **guilt**. Some people feel annoyed, **irritated**, or **frustrated**. It can also be a combination of emotions.

CHAPTER 2

WHY AM I GROUCHY?

There can be many reasons you feel grouchy. One could be that your needs are not being met. Not feeling safe, not being in control, and not getting attention or **support** are examples of needs not being met.

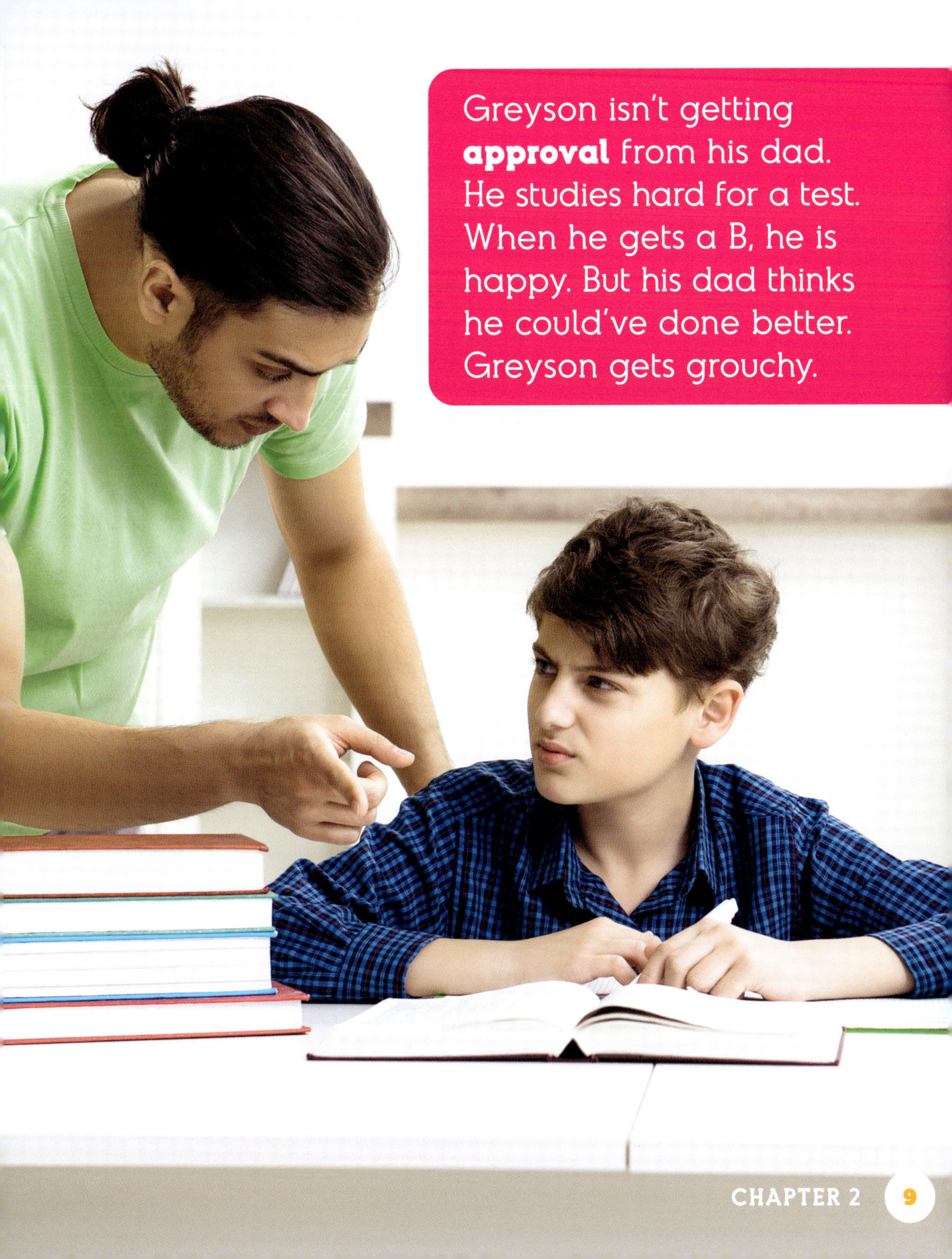

Greyson isn't getting **approval** from his dad. He studies hard for a test. When he gets a B, he is happy. But his dad thinks he could've done better. Greyson gets grouchy.

Another reason for grouchiness could be feeling **discouraged**. It can be hard to learn new things. You may feel like you are failing. This can make you grouchy.

Negative self-talk is a third reason. Olivia tells herself she isn't smart. The more she tells herself that, the grouchier she feels.

LISTEN TO YOUR BODY

Sensations in your body, such as hunger or sleepiness, can make you grouchy, too. Notice what your body is telling you. Maybe you need to eat a healthy snack or take a short break.

When you are grouchy, you might say things you don't mean. This can affect others.

Max is grouchy and can't make decisions. When his older sister **pressures** him, Max yells, "I hate you!" He doesn't mean it. It just came out. Now his sister feels sad.

CHAPTER 3

GROUCHINESS STEPS

Everyone feels grouchy sometimes. It is OK to feel grouchy. You don't have to run away from it. Sometimes you just have to feel the feeling. Let's learn how.

Step one is to **identify** your mood. Being **mindful** of your body sensations can help you do this. If you are grouchy, your muscles may clench and feel tight. You may feel tired. Your heart may beat fast.

Step two is to **acknowledge** your mood. Being grouchy feels bad, but it isn't harmful or wrong. It is a mood that will pass.

When you feel grouchy, you can say, "It's OK to feel this way. I will feel better. This feeling won't last forever."

TALK TO SOMEONE

If your grouchy mood doesn't go away, talk to an adult you trust. Let him or her know what you are feeling and when it started.

Step three is to question your mood. Was there an event or a thought that started it? Identifying how it started will make it less mysterious.

You can write in a journal to recognize patterns. Write down your feelings and how they started. You may find that you got frustrated at track practice, which put you in a bad mood.

Step four is to let yourself be grouchy. It doesn't have to ruin your day. Remember that everyone is grouchy sometimes. What will you do the next time you are grouchy?

AFTER THE STEPS

Once you have done the grouchiness steps, try to take your mind off your mood. Create something. Talk to a friend. Exercise. Do some deep breathing. See if any of these help you feel better!

GOALS AND TOOLS

GROW WITH GOALS

Being grouchy can make the day tough. There are things you can do to make the day easier. Try these goals to help with your mood.

Goal: Identify what you are feeling. Name your emotion and think about what might have started that feeling.

Goal: Draw a picture or create art that expresses what you are feeling.

Goal: Talk to a friend, a family member, or a trusted adult about what you are feeling. Ask if he or she has had similar feelings. What helps him or her feel better?

TRY THIS!

Journaling can help you process your feelings. Getting your thoughts on paper can help make them easier to manage. Don't worry about spelling or punctuation. Just write or draw what you are feeling. Expressing your thoughts can help you see how they started and help you talk about your feelings.

GLOSSARY

acknowledge
To recognize and accept the truth about something.

anxiety
A feeling of worry or fear.

approval
The belief that something is good or acceptable.

discouraged
Feeling a lack of courage or confidence.

emotion
A feeling, such as happiness, sadness, or anger.

frustrated
Annoyed or angry.

guilt
A feeling of having done something wrong.

identify
To recognize or tell what something or who someone is.

irritated
Feeling or showing slight anger or annoyance.

mindful
A mentality achieved by focusing on the present moment and calmly recognizing and accepting your feelings, thoughts, and sensations.

mood
An emotion that lasts longer than a few minutes.

negative self-talk
Words or thoughts to yourself that cause you to doubt yourself or your abilities and that limit your ability to believe in yourself.

pressures
Persuades someone to do something.

sensations
Particular feelings that your body experiences.

support
A source of comfort or encouragement.

TO LEARN MORE

FACT SURFER

Finding more information is as easy as 1, 2, 3.

1. Go to www.factsurfer.com
2. Enter "**Ifeelgrouchy**" into the search box.
3. Choose your book to see a list of websites.

INDEX

Blue Owl Books are published by Jump!, 5357 Penn Avenue South, Minneapolis, MN 55419, www.jumplibrary.com

Library of Congress Cataloging-in-Publication Data

Names: Finne, Stephanie, author.
Title: I feel grouchy / by Stephanie Finne.
Description: Minneapolis, MN: Jump!, Inc., [2022]
Series: States of mind | Includes index. | Audience: Ages 7–10
Identifiers: LCCN 2020048893 (print)
LCCN 2020048894 (ebook)
ISBN 9781636901022 (hardcover)
ISBN 9781636901039 (paperback)
ISBN 9781636901046 (ebook)
Subjects: LCSH: Temper–Juvenile literature. | Anger in children–Juvenile literature. | Emotions in children–Juvenile literature.
Classification: LCC BF723.A4 F56 2022 (print) | LCC BF723.A4 (ebook) | DDC 155.4/1247–dc23
LC record available at https://lccn.loc.gov/2020048893
LC ebook record available at https://lccn.loc.gov/2020048894

Editor: Eliza Leahy
Designer: Michelle Sonnek

Photo Credits: MAHATHIR MOHD YASIN/Shutterstock, cover; Gelpi/Shutterstock, 1; Creativa Images/Shutterstock, 3; WendellandCarolyn/iStock, 4; Viktoriia Hnatiuk/Shutterstock, 5; LightField Studios/Shutterstock, 6–7; Saturated/iStock, 8; Elnur/Shutterstock, 9; Prostock-studio/Shutterstock, 10–11; Pixel-Shot/Shutterstock, 12–13; Donna Ellen Coleman/Shutterstock, 14; Ursula Page/Shutterstock, 15; Odua Images/Shutterstock, 16–17; SeventyFour/Shutterstock, 18–19; PK Studio/Shutterstock, 20–21.

Printed in the United States of America at Corporate Graphics in North Mankato, Minnesota.